ADVANTAGES
OF BEING EVERGREEN

Recent Cleveland State University Poetry Center publications:

Poetry
The Hartford Book by Samuel Amadon
The Grief Performance by Emily Kendal Frey
My Fault by Leora Fridman
Orient by Nicholas Gulig
Stop Wanting by Lizzie Harris
Vow by Rebecca Hazelton
Age of Glass by Anna Maria Hong
The Tulip-Flame by Chloe Honum
Render / An Apocalypse by Rebecca Gayle Howell
A Boot's a Boot by Lesle Lewis
In One Form to Find Another by Jane Lewty
50 Water Dreams by Siwar Masannat
daughterrarium by Sheila McMullin
The Bees Make Money in the Lion by Lo Kwa Mei-en
Residuum by Martin Rock
Festival by Broc Rossell
The Firestorm by Zach Savich
Mother Was a Tragic Girl by Sandra Simonds
I Live in a Hut by S.E. Smith
Bottle the Bottles the Bottles the Bottles by Lee Upton
Adventures in the Lost Interiors of America by William D. Waltz
Uncanny Valley by Jon Woodward
You Are Not Dead by Wendy Xu

Essays
I Liked You Better Before I Knew You So Well by James Allen Hall
A Bestiary by Lily Hoang
The Leftovers by Shaelyn Smith

Translation
I Burned at the Feast: Selected Poems of Arseny Tarkovsky translated by Philip Metres and
    Dimitri Psurtsev

For a complete list of titles visit www.csupoetrycenter.com

ADVANTAGES
OF BEING EVERGREEN

Oliver Baez Bendorf

Cleveland State University Poetry Center
Cleveland, Ohio

Printed in the United States of America
Printed on acid-free paper

ISBN: 978-1-880834-00-8

First edition

23   22   21   20   19   5   4   3   2   1

This book is published by the Cleveland State University Poetry Center,
2121 Euclid Avenue, Cleveland, Ohio 44115-2214
www.csupoetrycenter.com and is distributed by
SPD / Small Press Distribution, Inc. www.spdbooks.org.

Cover image: "Beach Instinct, 2017," Wyatt Hersey
Cover design: Amy Freels
Interior cover image: "Ghost Ship Collage," Oliver Baez Bendorf
Advantages of Being Evergreen was designed and typeset by Amy Freels in Adobe Garamond
Pro with Mr. Eaves Sans display.

A catalog record for this title is available from the Library of Congress.

FOR KIM

I kept abandoning the world.
It kept calling me back.

—NATHANIEL MACKEY

CONTENTS

FIELD GUIDE

When you arrive, it must be morning. The light must blue over triangles of treeline. There must be fields of corn and there must be coroners mistaking elbow joint for knee bone. There must be a trail and there must be the skull of a possum still lodged inside the trunk of a tree. There must be a tree. There must be the slightest hint of danger. There must be corners neatly tucked. There must be red the color of a puppy's tongue, there must be pleasure strapped or stolen, and there must be ice there must always always always always be ice. There must be a way to feel our way toward the water and light from darkness. There must be fire. There must be a little candle thing that makes the bells go 'round. There must be a girl, there has always been a girl. There must be a boy, there has always been a boy. There has never been a man but there must now be a man, not because one is needed but because one isn't. There must be a ghost. They must be hungry. There must be pine needles. Papercuts. A punchline. A burial. There must be a way to fall asleep beside the dead coyote and not wake up wearing its fur. There must be a horseman. There must be someone around here who remembers the voice of the girl. It isn't me, but it must be me. There must be daylight. There must be a yellow house. There must be a window. A ladder. A compass. We must have new names. There must be a boy and a girl and we must have new names. There must be a boy and there must be a girl. There must be. There must be. There must be someone looking for us by now. They must wonder where we are.

EVERGREEN

What still grows in winter?
Fingernails of witches and femmes,
green moss on river rocks
lit with secrets. I let myself
go near the river but not
the railroad: this is my bargain.
Water boils in a kettle in the woods
and I can hear the train grow louder
but I also can't, you know?
Then I'm shaving in front of
an unbreakable mirror while a nurse
watches over my shoulder.
Damn. What still grows in winter?
Lynda brought me basil I crushed
with my finger and thumb just to
smell the inside. So I go
to the river but not the rail-
road, think I'll live another year.
River rock digs into my shoulders
like a lover who knows I don't want
power. I release every muscle against
the rock, give it all my warmth.
                              Snow shakes
onto my chest quick as table salt.
Branches above me full of pine needles
whip: when the river rock is done
with me, I could belong to the evergreen.
Safety is a rock I throw into the river.
My body is ready. I don't even think
a train runs through this town anymore.

RAIN AND TICKS IN TENNESSEE

felt like punishment, but for what?
Billay who was clenching his jaw
came around early, climbed in
bed with us.

No one had confessed
a thing, so what was all this
rain for? We went to Hardee's
for biscuits, drank

coffee among men
who I thought wore
so obvious
a desire for queer blood, but

which way did they
want it? To fuck or kill,
maybe both, and in what order?
Maybe they didn't

notice us at all, my nails
as blue as Billay's eyes,
shorts short as a question,
Daddy asking Billay

about his new man
in the next town and
how they fuck, and I swear
the whole Hardee's listened.

But maybe they didn't.
Maybe they didn't care at all.
Billay stopped the car
to pick wildflowers.

The lake was more like a slick
of water on mud and rock. Swarms
of swallowtails, so many swallow-
tails. We spread our towels

on a sandbar, offered our naked
bodies to the sky.
They swam, I read poems.
We crushed a tick that had

followed us to our slice
of paradise for our blood.
Life was beautiful *and* kind
for a moment that passed quick

as a storm. Back in town, Daddy
rubbed gravestones onto paper.
I got high under a tree,
watched a dog watching

me. Billay and Daddy pulled
confederate flags out of the
ground—why didn't I help?
Back on land,

we took family portraits
wearing animal masks. Billay
and Daddy burned the flags.
There was a darkness rising

up even though no one had
confessed anything. More like
why all this rain, all these ticks?
Earth not even buried

in the earth. So many gay
bodies on fire, offerings to
gods who don't deserve us,
gods of punishment, gods of plight.

The land in the holler weeps.
Still we dream of sanctuary,
follow a hand-drawn map
up the mountain.

ORACLE

sorry I missed your message, I
   have no excuse except the kava
      numbed my tongue again

(sure, only for a moment)

honestly felt I was deep under
   water—awash in sunlight's move-
      ments through canopy birch

I have come to the playground

to work (yes it seems I have this
   backward)—children in neckties
      sort papers on a bench, why?

I think I have come back,

already, as something else.
   what am I still doing in this park,
      pockets full of coconut meat,

scars where my breasts

were? dear fish bones, dear
   open hose, today I am a static channel
      carrying the weight of logic.

AFTER A WHILE, WE STOP ASKING

                    sometimes
on our saddest days, the river

lift up almost to the bridge.
on our saddest days, the river
on the bridge:
           river we build,
river swell up to the belly.

on our worst days, we stop
asking. we brown/white as one

body again
in fields of moon snow.
                    we assemble (fields of stubble, fields of thread).

because we've known
ourselves as throwaways
                    already,

we do not dispose. *kept*   we say

           and we mean it.

RITUAL

Even the yellow rose, the lake, even earth.
Life—not days strung together. The fire, the clearing.
Know what I mean? Rocks, Carlos's fist, my body—
everything was a circle.

Our thighs was cold as rocks circling the river.
Snow covered the meat. Carlos.
We lit cherry wood. With Carlos's arrow, we

      shot
      new
      constell-
      ations
      into
      the
      sky
        (believing
            that
            new
            ones
            were
            possible)—

flies circled us faster

                      throughout the
day and night. The kind of clearing where my breasts
was unmistakable.   Some of us was quiet
in our skin until some of us was barefoot,

some of us faded into the
boulders with no sound—my whole life rose up,
ghosts into flame.

                                        Vultures

circle overhead while we dig

for fossils, not of us. I bring a vial.
Someone breaks the seal. The smoke
feels warm, almost loving.

                    We fly all night.

FIRE STARTS FROM THE UNDERSIDE

after visiting Idyll Dandy Arts (IDA) in Tennessee

We practiced cutting down a tree.
                    Held the ax,
held our breath, we watched it fall
                    across a creek. We needed
a bridge.

We had been many years
without one and we needed one.

We all practiced gathering things. We
showed one another our piles. There
was water. Birds all black, with maybe
a head shaped like this: [redacted]

Held hands before each meal.
Did and did not want to share.

            I wore the fox's face
                    to the family pictures. You
                            were a lamb and a bear.

YOU WEAR BLAZE ORANGE WHEN YOU LEAVE THE CITY

The hunter
is a difficult
woman
to hold
when she holds
a bow and arrow.

Smells like cedar
in the bed we share

because
she keeps, under the mattress,

the stars—
a flickering map.

BREATH I

almost alone animal away
become bed begin behind believe
benign billay black bridge burning
calls care carlos carry
circle clear confess daddy
days drink earth egg else
empty face fall family float follow
fuck full function ghost
grows haunted held hold
holy hungry knees knows
lake leaves life live
maybe mercy mine
monster moon
mother nice nothing past
paternal pine practice prayer
pull queer quiet rain salt shaking
shape shiny sin singing
sits sky sleep small soft
sometimes sound
stop things took
toward tree turned voice
wake wanted watch
whole wild wilderness winter
wishes witch wooden
woods write wrong

DEAR RANE ARROYO

I thought I wanted to be everything all at once.
Poet that sits on a bucket in the dunes and the bucket
    too. Blowjob too. Monster on my knees.

                    Everything all at once:
    river behind you holy. River behind you comes. I speak
        with your voice now—you tilt open my windpipe.

        Of all the ways to enter. Let it be through the throat.

ELEGY

see my self
reflected in both
beard and lace

on the dark
window lakeside
insects provide

      ambient

      far
from the girl
I was

I left because
everyone did

GHOST SHIP NOVENA INSIDE A YEAR-LONG FUNERAL

December 5, 2016: a fire breaks out at the Ghost Ship collective warehouse in Oakland, taking the lives of thirty-six working artists, musicians, and scholars, many of whom were queer and trans.

my god my god our prayer go—nine fucking days dios mío dios mío dios mío
my god my god my god my god my god (that was how we pray) (all we knew)

nine days we drift downstream like that, count prayers on a rip-rap rosary—

fire, you

good for nothing mother

               fucker   all you do is burn—

drained of salt, we let eddies rock

us bank to bank

KNOT: A GATHERING

bright morning hollow throats (we hunger)
bundles of ice dyed in the river (we dyed in the river all the time)
nailbed of the claw we grew together (broke it)
salt cakes from our tears
whoooosh of "we" on exhale
every single bioavailable nutrient
calico ribbon
not the skunk but its gallop into black
teeth of our dead around our neck

TEXTURE OF NEEDING BROWN

after "Texture of Needing Yellow" by Sawako Nakayasu. Johnson, VT.

I learn from a study that brown is the least loved color in the western world. I look for brown among white, I feel browner, I practice—

Needing Brown as a composition of wholeness, or a grove.
Needing Brown the way my mother do, sideways.
Needing Brown as a love practice.
The sound of Needing Brown and its vibration through the hardwood.
Desiring Brown on Brown on Brown on Brown.
Needing Brown as the idea of a thing left alone.
Mulatto on cowback in winter. Slop in the pen.
The appetite of Needing Brown—as a growl.
The prayer of Needing Brown, as incantation.
Or insistence on being Needed as a dirty thing.

PAPI LOVES ME LIKE A VIOLET, OR A PIÑATA

                                        I want to be
loved
for
            color   and smell—

        how long I take to open.

                                everyone is okay
with this and says so—
we can do anything

            in yellow.

                                        —so how long I take to open?

            just look, you said.
                                        look.

MY BODY THE HAUNTED HOUSE

This house is haunted you know. Someone died in here. Where is the basement of the body I don't know. Where is the attic I don't know. I carry her around with me. Stillborn in my boy-womb. There was a girl died young no funeral. A haunted house is always alone. People come to be scared because they like it they like to be scared knowing they can leave anytime and they do they always do they always leave. Back to their safe and warm without me, I mean the house. A haunted house is always alone. I carry your body (in my body). I live for both of us now. Cannot pinpoint what I miss. Looking for the chicken exit. Desire wrapped in a sheet. Where is the body I said I don't know. No body no case everyone knows that. Am I free to go now. I want to go home. I said I want to go.

LONG SHOT WITH A GIRL WHO IS ALSO ME

Mountains. Trail on
loop. Somedays I re-
member the girl out of me.
Remember my bed, pushed
close against the wall—
along the train tracks,
the road, losing my
coming lights, unable to.

I have paid for this:
to fall out of the sky and
dream my scars away.
Breasts have grown in
the river. In my dreams
come trick candles. I
give all my wishes
and they come right
back. Dark room, now
nerves catching fire.
For an hour my nipples
recline on a white
table. I sleep.

My parents wanted
winter past the moun-
tains, a perfect closed
flame as a beating.
Why can't I remember

the girl out of me? I go
up all the way,
it was almost.
I too have walked
on the side of
coming headlights,
unable to look
away.

I THINK I'VE ALREADY COME BACK AS SOMETHING ELSE

it was rainy there
were a few planks lined up over a
gutter of mud washed up between
car and shed

daylight nothing but a yellow crevice

otherwise darkness

haven't we
been here before—

don't we know this part already?

in the presence of all these

grey herons
coming through an open sky

everything falls away

attention narrows only to sensation

someone cries and someone comes
back and someone else eats
part of a partly rotten apple.

BREATH I, I

act aids already animal arms around arroyo
asking atop attention away badlands beard bed bedtime behind belly
biscuits bled blood blowjob blue bodies boy
bridge bucket buried burned burrs candy car care carry cash cheeks circle
clenching climbed clings coffee comes communicate conductor
confessed congregate conifers creeps crevice crushed cry daddy
darkness daylight deserve design desire display dog drank dream
driftwood drop dunes dusty ears earth easier eats else enter
everything extra eyes faggot falls family felt finger
fire fix flags fleeing float flush foliage follow fuck full fur gay
gods gravestones grey ground guide gutter gym hallway
haunted headlights hemlock heron hold holler holy honestly horn howl
hurts ink island jaw kept kill knee knew lake land lava leans leaves
life line listened litter love lucky mammal man map maple mark
masks maybe meet memory metal moonbeam morning moss
mountain mud nails naked narrows needles night note nothing obvious
offered oil onto open order otherwise paper parade paradise partly passed
pedal piano pick pile planks playground plight poke pour prepare
punishment queer question quick rain read red request
rickety rise river road rock rosewater rotten round rubbed rum rusty
sanctuary sandbar scat scrubby self sensation shed shift short sidewalk sits sky slice
slick smack smash smell sniff sock soft someone something speak spider
splinter spreads sprouts stay stick stopped stored storm sun-up swallow
swam swarm swear tails tells ten tennessee thank thighs think
thought thread throat throws thru ticks tilt tissue tongue took toward towels
town trailer train trash tree turf universe utility veil vein voice wanted washed
water weep whole whose windpipe

FAGGOT TURF

Daddy and me
prepare for winter.
Late at night tells
me how to care

for conifers. We poke
our dusty thighs with
needles, we pour
ink into the holes—

hemlock and lava rock,
make ourselves
a universe that way
in the passenger car.

Conductor leans
on the horn—
one long note
of a rusty piano.

Haunted by us too,
he throws the word
out his window like
litter and we *faggots!*

catch it.

QUEER IN THE ALMOST-SOUTH

Bloomington Community Orchard, Indiana

van squeaked
as it turned
off the road

its headlights
eyes of something
living

       (more like
a squeal, insistent)

sun was down
though it wasn't
late

       I was

       high
in the orchard
Ross tends

and sure
the van meant
trouble

I slipped

down a black
trail toward
rotted out
birch
after
an owl
a man

told me be there

feeling watched
from where?

god, maybe
pileated woodpecker maybe—

mercy mercy mercy

mercy on us all

DREAM

The staplers looked like confetti I tell her and I can tell by the look on her face that the sudden plurality of staplers begs an explanation. In fact there was a whole haphazardry of them floating on a white surface, each a different color brightly lit. Like jelly beans yes or confetti I said or fruit. Then what? Well I feel excited that they are mine. The staplers she says in a way that is not exactly a question but not not so I say yes the staplers glad they're mine. There is one in particular and I reach for it. This is always the case: one thing in particular, me reaching for it. What else? This one is red. Swingline. What? Swingline and she writes this on her yellow pad. A red Swingline and when I take it in my hand it's wavy like silicone sort of looks like a dildo like it might be nice to fuck with. Good handle. Nice shape. Even in my nice dream my stapler is the dick I don't have and some part of me wants to say sorry to ruin everything but the red one I reached for was sexy raw like meat so I'm not sorry at all.

WHO STITCHED THE ROAD TOGETHER

Maybe I looked, to the god,

    like gentle meat. Maybe he

saw me inside out—not collision,

    but desire for collision. His next

antlerless kill—and I wanted it.

    Tender of his crosshairs.

Blur of high beam. He accelerated.

    Spat rain onto my ankles.

Though I have not been

    good, I felt good. His head

spun like a doll's head. I did not run.

THIS MULTITUDE WE'VE BECOME

funny thing
is I feel more
girl now than
ever before. walk
with hips, not
wish they'd be-
come invisible.
why'd it take
me so long
to get here?

I wish for
all of us
bearded mon-
sters to know
we can be
soft too, loved too.

RAINWATER FROM CERTAIN ENCHANTED STREAMS

After the foxes come, I wake, put on a self.
Sometimes still get *ma'am* on the phone (never *miss*).
Some friends call me fairy, dyke, & I'm all these things.
Cosmically I count seconds between my thighs (still thick)
and lightning. I inject, grow a beard, bleed awhile… I become my wildest self
through make-believe—to the river with this thunderous me: carrier and
     carried
both, everything else a tenderness held with string until it becomes my face
     entirely.
Me suckling through my own prow, family of foxes making yips & howls the
     others can hear
emanating from the woods.

RIVER I DREAM ABOUT

Moon river, swollen river, river of starhole
and bright, harness river, lichen river,
river we velvet with our filth.
River of butter and river of witches, river
cracked open careful like egg, or burst
apart, unleashing its violet load.
River mouths, river beds, every back
forty creek, every crick, made of
trickles, made of synth, river of sound
as vibration, river where we all get free.
River that curve down a backbone.
River through which I particle heat.
Feathery and wet, lemony and loud,
river that still smells skin, browned
around a neck, softened with sweat.
River you wear tight on your hips,
given in private, or out in the open.

River I dream about. River from the inside.
River where we shouts the feeling.

Septum river, bundle river, river of mercy, sometimes edging so far into
    night the moon goes
                              (whoosh)   dark.

Yes, all night river, burnt sugar river.
We pull the river into our bellies, we
go out walking. We river in darkness

as entire paw prints of color and light.
Everything rivers in motion. River
of holy, river of freaks, river where
my fur belong to me. Softer than
it seem river. Honey and Vaseline river.
Brown river, black river, off the map river.
I will be there, printing textures of rock
on the skin of me, belly down, face down.
My god, it is good to be home.

EVERYTHING HURTS IN A GOOD WAY

does every animal
                   communicate
                              the way
                         my tongue
               hurts?

I go to the river I was under,

I make the

                   river

red

*

does it get easier

I go to the river

I make the burrs

congregate

     fur clings

          to my dream self
in the river,
more rosewater
      down the   vein.

*

          dream—was there rain?

honestly I felt too much.

(mark me with a pile of
    the bad ones)

everything hurts
about listening

hurts
in a good way

I try to make the pile of
                    love me

            fur clings
                                    like
        the river,   in a good way.
tell me about

*

                    bodies
                where they meet
write about what goes in circles

                    junkyard
                    tributaries

                                stick my finger

                            for
            animal design

            scat display of driftwood

sniff metal
                        at the edge of

                bedtime.
        boy

                        makes
                        island under the bridge

*

does every animal cry out?

I go to the river

(my guides guide me)

red round memory stored in
                        chest, tissue gone

36

*

rain drips off
roof of the old

           drive

                 mud rocks

                    long time

                    long long time

for the memories.

        tissue   been

        the only
        thread.

BREATH I, I, I

according afraid amen backpack bad bank
beautiful better birch bit blood boat bones bread
break breasts breath bright
bucket campsite candle car case cast catch
chest child children clean clings clinical collective creek
daylight dead deck died dig dios dirty doctor dogs
door drive drop ear easy
eat end enough enter entire
evergreen everybody eyes fallen feed feet
floor fly forgive foxes
front funeral getting given
glass glory goat goods green
ground guide hair hallway
handle happens hard head headlight hear
heaven hello hole hope hour hurts ice knew
knot leads leg lift line lit lonely longer lose lost
louder lover map meant meat memory middle mind
mío moment mud mustache nails
needle news nightmare note offers orange
papi paradise particular
paw people pictures pile
playground please pleasures
poem poke possible prairie pray
pumpkin races reach read
relate return review riding rooster rope round rub sang sauna
saying scars seat seem sensation sense
shape ship short shot shoulders sign skin
smaller snow son sort soup

speak stars starts steep
students study sun table
takes tears tells texture
thank thick thought throat ticks
tiny tips today top track train triangle under
vibration walls warm weeks wolf wonder

OTHER NAMES

*They call the mountain Carlos because
it is brown, although its purple slopes
at dusk suggest other names.*
—Ray Gonzalez

Papi, grapefruit, anchor—every
week Carlos comes with gifts
in his dirty white sedan.

He texts from unknown
numbers. Some weeks tall
other weeks not. Carlos

buries mice in the woods
goes careful with their
brittle tails. Carlos digs

holes the size of his fist—
Daddy to the land also.
Brown mud, the rocks the river softened

and the river also. Rock
also. Boot crunch. River
of ice the bridge crosses

and the bridge also.
Kind of togetherness
we make with desire

to lose our voice
to the river. Hum
tenderness

to the edge where listening
is no longer possible—
go beyond it.

THE CARP

Its scales lifted, like rainbows, from ice.

Tail bent back against flesh—kite of bones.

The head was buried under snow.

Something scraped the belly.

God, I thought you hated me. The self

deflates. Should I have stayed at home

and thought of the lake?

Pinecone made of scales…

feeling lucky again. Whoooo-wee!

Lord, if it is you, command

me to come on the water.

Or is it only a falcon this time?

Or is that witch who lives above

the barbecue joint with all those

wind chimes? Or is it Rane.

Or any other blood I come from

or mix with.

We stand upon it, each touching

each. Summer's dock made to wait on shore.

Moonrise plunk of buzz-dive

and whatever sings from feral pines.

The whole skin a pile of firewood.

The heart a distant geode.

WHO SPIT INTO THE PUMPKIN, WHO THEY WAITING FOR

No rooster in town, at least not in earshot. A pumpkin
decomposes on the bank, and I know to bring a lover
back you need five nails of a rooster before you cast a pumpkin
into the river. I have given up, I think, on unrestricted love, but not
the search. Something happens under the bridge. I come up singing.
The egg was the easy part, with all the hens. Pepper, marjoram, easy.
But those rooster nails … I wait years. I wait my entire life. No one
teaches a mother spell, but isn't that what every spell is for?

What I want from the river is what I always want:
to be held by a stronger thing that, in the end, chooses mercy.

BOONDOCK

turned my back on
the lake after
the first time it
froze on me

guess I'd already
lost that ticket
that would get us
out of here

been seeing
bats at early
hours almost

daylight—I sing
without words
already lost that

ticket

and stretches
of stillness on the
tin can rope

like nights without
sunrise lake
breeze between
our windows

free lumber
on the outskirts
nightly emissions

to the moon
soft as a boy can
be and even

softer when the
mood was right

giving up some
fucks and my fur
is the worst
of me greeting
the harvest

and going some-
where together
I go out

for a drive on my
own solo
at the wheel

everything
vibrates

at this
speed—Papi
I'm doing much

better at
feeling alive
and moving

through it
day by day

small pleasures
which
are the bright-

est treasures
in this dark-
ness

WEB

Black rat bones, brown dog
hair, bottom of a bucket. Salt. Water
thick with sulfur. Dust gathered from
a graveyard on the hill.   We decide
our ancestors must love our queerness
now that they are dead (but of course
they might not).   Smoke
          lifts the four corners.
No one has a tarantula, so we
use a common spider, found missing half
its limbs. Onion root, oil lamp,
cinnamon sticks, bathwater.
We pour honey into a goddess
cup (no one has a bull horn)—
watch it drip out of range.

I think we are clean now.

I think we are ready.

SOME OF US FULL MOON HEARTS

wept one another to sleep just to hear
      something like the river again—not

          knowing our tears was the river
                which we had left in body

                    old wild sounds
                        become barnboard

WITCH KEPT

me on the road.
sun-up in
the Badlands—

flush rises
to my cheeks.

scrubby foliage,
beard I cash in on,
fur that creeps down

my belly and out
my thighs—I become

a wolf so that I may
speak to
my grandmother

on the road. I love
a witch who says the veil

is thin.
Daddy sprouts moss
in Olympia.

some nights moon
a lantern full of oil.

these night-
mares where I
flee the bad mammal,

who stays
silent. my students and I

fix our
ears toward
the hall.

lucky to be kept by
my witch in morning,

witch down by
the lake with an extra
seat for me.

over the lake,
moonbeams reach

and reach for me,
spider arms smack
me over whose knee,

and I howl.

WE CONGREGATE

sons of beaches, glitter tongues, sister hoods, hermanos,
faggots, wolverines—everything under the moon.

THE EARTH IS MY HOME

at Short Mountain Sanctuary in Tennessee

Big Dipper don't want my tears
and it sends them right back to me.
Someone offers salt, someone
nurses firewood. We rub it in.
Then a choke of eucalyptus on air.
A man chants on a bench.
Soft, like he's putting a baby to sleep.
We follow him to his garden,
all three of us in the front seat.
The earth is my home and there is
much to cry about. It always helps
to look up, look all the way up,

look up, look up, look up, we look
                up, up, up.

NOTES & ACKNOWLEDGMENTS

This project began at Vermont Studio Center in November 2016—I'm grateful to all the writers, artists, and staff who exchanged ideas and creative energy in that tense post-election dawn. For fellowship in all senses of the word, which allowed me to begin again. Some of you gave me feedback on early drafts: Willie Perdomo, Shamala Gallagher, Shanita Bigelow, Halsey Rodman.

After Vermont, I put my belongings in a storage unit and drove across the country and back. Many people offered food, shelter, and other loving assistance along the way: the Rhodes-Chang family in Washington, D.C., Suzanne Gold and Allison Crowley in Baltimore, Amy Peterson and Robinberg Acres in Western Massachusetts, Elijah Edelman and Jason Terry in Providence, Mom, Dad, Ani and Jason in Colorado, Della, Erik, and Maddie in Olympia, Jim in Montana and his lockout kit, the Senchyne-Fielders in Wisconsin, Ross Gay in Indiana, Billy and Bella in Cincinnati, Billay and Bear in Tennessee, Heather Renèe and Chris in Williamsburg, Adrienne and Matt in Connecticut, Jesse Lee and Dan in Madison. There are others and I'm grateful to you all.

To my students at Wisconsin and Kalamazoo. Special thanks and tenderness to Thunderpuff, Rosedrop, Cricketcliff, Figtwist, Sparklestripe, Cosmotwig, Parsleyhorn, Hollyfoam, Tangleflip, Dimplemint, Pinewhistle, and Glitterbug, as I finished this manuscript.

About rivers, what Willie told me: sometimes you go it alone, sometimes you need a guide. My teacher for a lifetime is Lynda Barry, to whom I owe my life. Amaud Jamaul Johnson has sustained me with support and friendship—thank you for everything. Rane Arroyo's spirit and work was a gentle presence as I wrote. Gabrielle Calvocoressi, how lucky I am to be alive at the same time as you, pal—thanks for believing in me. CAConrad's life and work: for modeling bravery to be a queer body, and poetry as a ritual act. Jen Chang, your nurture, friendship, and guidance has meant so very much. Jon Senchyne, there for me through thick and thin: thank you, thank you.

CantoMundo, University of Wisconsin-Madison, PEN Writers' Fund, Kalamazoo College: I am grateful for your support at various stages of this book project.

Dr. Beverly Fischer and her staff in Maryland, and all who tended to me from near and far, Temim Fruchter most of all, in my recovery from top surgery after five years of binding my chest. I still feel drunk on oxygen and all it makes possible.

Alex Smith, Wo Chan, Meg Day: you are family and I'm buoyed by your mere existence, not to mention your brilliance and heart. As well, my friendships from Washington, D.C., have been a dear gift I carried through this book, in creativity and resistance. My studiomates from Everyday Gay Holiday in Madison, where I finished the manuscript: KC Councilor, Cate Barry, Finn Enke, Sylvia Johnson, Tia Clark, and Kim Charles Kay. Sami Schalk. Roger and Lou at Design Coalition: thank you for opening your space to our dreams. To my fellow Wisconsin Institute for Creative Writing Fellows, 2017-2018: Tiana Clark, Tia Clark, Leila Chatti, Marta Evans—for boogaloo and mutually assured vulnerability. Derrick, you too. And all who made that year so special.

M. Milks, Trevor Dane Ketner, Kristen Stone, and Wren Hanks each have read individual poems or earlier drafts of the manuscript, and offered insightful feedback.

Gratitude to Cleveland State University Poetry Center, and Caryl Pagel in particular, as well as the judges of the Open Book Competition, for seeing this work, giving it form, and helping me let it go!

Some lines in "The Carp" channel Elizabeth Bishop's poems "The Fish" and "Questions of Travel." In the same poem, the phrase "feral pines" is meant as homage to Feral Pines, who was a bass player and transgender woman who died in the Ghost Ship fire. She was 29.

My partner, Kim Charles Kay, is my fellow traveler and best editor. I'm grateful for the life we share and the learning and teaching between us. It's a joy every day to be gay with you.

Living kin on all my sides, much love. Ancestors, spirits, guides, and allies: thank you for looking out for me. Biggest thanks of all to the land, and all the plants and animals. And thanks to you.

The book's epigraph is from Nathaniel Mackey's *Lay Ghost*.

Gratitude to the editors and publishers of the following magazines, in which these poems—sometimes in different versions—originally appeared:

Academy of American Poets/*Poem-a-Day*: "Evergreen"

American Poetry Review: "River I Dream About," "After A While," "Faggot Turf," "Some of Us Full Moon Hearts"

Black Warrior Review: "Ritual"

BOAAT Journal: "Ghost Ship Novena Inside a Year-Long Funeral"

diode: "Field Guide"

Foglifter: "Girl Who Is Also Me," "Elegy"

Ninth Letter: "Texture of Needing Brown," "Who Spit into the Pumpkin, Who They Waiting For"

Poetry Northwest: "Witch Kept," "Fire Starts from the Underside," "Other Names"

Sycamore Review: "My Body the Haunted House"

Third Coast: "Rain and Ticks in Tennessee"

West Branch: "The Carp," "Web"

Oliver Baez Bendorf is the author of a previous collection, *The Spectral Wilderness*, and a chapbook, *The Gospel According to X*. His poems have appeared in *American Poetry Review*, *BOMB*, *Poem-a-Day*, *Poetry*, *Troubling the Line: Trans and Genderqueer Poetry and Poetics*, and elsewhere. Born and raised in Iowa, he is an assistant professor of poetry at Kalamazoo College in Michigan.